OH TOTO!
WHERE DID YOU GO?

BY JONATHAN HALL

ILLUSTRATIONS BY CAROL RUZICKA

Oh Toto!
Where Did You Go?

by Jonathan Hall

Book design, layout, and all illustrations by Carol Ruzicka.

Story font set in Nobility Casual with Crumb as title and cover font.

Printed in the United States of America

For more information about this book visit www.Totothetornadokitten.com

Follow Toto on Facebook at TototheTornadoKitten

978-0-615-78845-6

First Edition **2013**

♥

This book is
for anyone
who's pet has also
been their
best friend.

♥

To CAMERON –
HAPPY BIRTHDAY FROM TOTO!

ToTo Loves Birthday Cake!

ToTo

x

When I woke up this morning,

I knew something was wrong,

the bed side was empty,

my friend Toto was gone.

He had packed up his leash,

and taken some food,

but left not a note,

which I thought was quite rude.

I set out to find him,

I'd search high and low,

"Oh Toto," I thought,

"where on earth did you go?"

I stopped at the coffeehouse,

which was quite near.

I asked the nice lady

"Has Toto been here?"

"Oh yes!" She said smiling.

"Humm. . . let me see. . .

Oh now I remember—

He had catnip tea!"

He had been in for breakfast,

then finished his snack.

He said his goodbyes

and slipped right out the back.

My friends at the bank

said he'd brought in some change.

"A cat at the bank?" cried one lady,

"How Strange!"

He deposited some cash—

three dimes and a dollar.

"Give the money to the shelter,"

read the note tucked in his collar.

The tellers gave him some treats,

while he sat on the floor.

Then he got up and stretched

and went right out the door.

The fireman said

he had stopped in to chat.

"That's no ordinary pet there,

he's our mascot cat!"

"The first time we met him,

He was so tiny and small,

but look at him now.

So handsome and tall!"

He had helped out with chores,

and sat with them all.

But when the fire bell rang,

he went out on a call!

At the nice nursing home,

he sat with Nanas and Grandpas,

next to wheelchairs and walkers,

sitting pretty on all paws.

They cooed and they chatted,

they spoiled him rotten,

and showing his thanks,

he rubbed each with his noggin!

"Thanks for having me by,

I'll come back quite soon.

I have to head out

for an appointment at noon."

The librarian told me

he'd stopped in for a look.

He sat with the children

while they read him his book.

It was the story of a kitten

blown into a tree.

And all the people who helped him

until he came home with me.

When story time was over

he said, "I've places to be!"

He cleaned off his whiskers

"I'm going to be on TV."

The Postmaster told me

he had brought in some mail.

There were so many packages

even one tied to his tail!

He mailed out his books,

to each Toto fan.

To Vermont and to Boston

and even Japan!

When the books were all sent,

he thanked them a bunch.

Then headed back out

to meet someone for lunch!

The whole school was there

when he arrived on the bus.

An appearance by Toto,

always causes a fuss!

He taught each of the students

about being kind to their pets.

How important it is

to treat all with respect.

He wandered through classrooms

then sat for a spell.

And left on a mission,

at the sound of the bell.

He remarked to his friends,

at the YMCA,

"Visiting the gym

is the best part of my day!"

He watched people stretch,

lift things, and run.

"Silly Humans," he thought,

"Cats do all that for fun!"

After doing cat Yoga,

He strolled out the door.

"Thanks for the workout—

I'll be back soon for more!"

He had gotten a ride
to the television station,
so he could tell his great story
to all Toto Nation.

Sitting upright and proud
he'd talked to the host.
What a very special tale—
You're the cat with the most!

"Thanks for giving me time
to share my great story.
But I have to head out now
I'm really quite sorry!"

By the end of the day,

I was sad and alone.

Still missing my best friend,

I headed back home.

But when I got to the house

and opened the door,

I found Toto quite happy,

asleep on the floor.

"Of all the places I went,

when I got out to roam," he said,

"I found the best place to be,

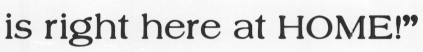
is right here at HOME!"

23

About The Author

After the successful release of the first book, Jonathan decided that there was even more to Toto's story and thus a second book was born. Between shifts as a Paramedic, he plays the role of chauffer to Toto driving him to his many appearances at schools, libraries, nursing homes and even birthday parties. Jonathan and Amy, his wife, continue to be amazed at how one tiny cat can mean so much more to so many people and help to heal a community.

About Toto

Despite having raised so much money on his first book, stardom has not gone to Toto's head. He remains just a regular cat, doing all the things cats like to do. He continues to enjoy car rides to visit his many fans and has made over 150 different appearances since his book release. Toto loves to promote healthy eating for both cats and humans and has recently developed an affinity for cucumbers and lettuce. If you are in Brimfield stop by the bank, where you will often see him hanging out with his friends. To find out where he is follow him on Facebook at Toto The Tornado Kitten.

About The Illustrator

If a picture tells 1000 words, then the Toto book series should be novels. Carol Ruzicka has captured the spirit of Toto so well, and her illustrations have bought the praise of both children and adults alike. She continues her work as an artist working from her studio in Vermont. Visit her website at www.carolruzicka.com